THE GREAT DEPRESSION

BY JOHN O'MARA

Gareth Stevens PUBLISHING

CRASHCOURSE

Please visit our website, www.garethstevens.com. For a free color catalog of all our high-quality books, call toll free 1-800-542-2595 or fax 1-877-542-2596.

Library of Congress Cataloging-in-Publication Data

Names: O'Mara, John, author.
Title: The Great Depression / John O'Mara.
Description: New York : Gareth Stevens Publishing, [2020] | Series: A look at US history | Includes index.
Identifiers: LCCN 2019012451| ISBN 9781538248751 (pbk.) | ISBN 9781538248775 (library bound) | ISBN 9781538248768 (6 pack)
Subjects: LCSH: Depressions--1929--United States--Juvenile literature. | United States--History--1919-1933--Juvenile literature. | United States--History--1933-1945--Juvenile literature.
Classification: LCC HB3717 1929 .O43 2020 | DDC 330.973/0916--dc23
LC record available at https://lccn.loc.gov/2019012451

First Edition

Published in 2020 by
Gareth Stevens Publishing
111 East 14th Street, Suite 349
New York, NY 10003

Editor: Therese Shea

Photo credits: Series art Christophe BOISSON/Shutterstock.com; (feather quill) Galushko Sergey/Shutterstock.com; (parchment) mollicart-design/Shutterstock.com; cover, p. 1 New York Times Co./Archive Photos/Getty Images; p. 5 Syda Productions/ Shutterstock.com; p. 7 Doucefleur/Shutterstock.com; p. 9 courtesy of the Library of Congress; p. 11 Library of Congress/Corbis Historical/Getty Images; p. 13 AFP/Getty Images; p. 15 Frederic Lewis/Archive Photos/Getty Images; p. 17 Hohum/Wikipedia Commons; p. 19 Library of Congress/Wikipedia Commons; p. 21 General Photographic Agency/Hulton Archive/Getty Images; p. 23 Bettmann/Getty Images; pp. 25, 27 Historical/Corbis Historical/Getty Images; p. 29 PNA Rota/Hulton Archive/Getty Images.

Printed in the United States of America

CPSIA compliance information: Batch #CW20GS: For further information contact Gareth Stevens, New York, New York at 1-800-542-2595.

CONTENTS

Words in the glossary appear in **bold** type the first time they are used in the text.

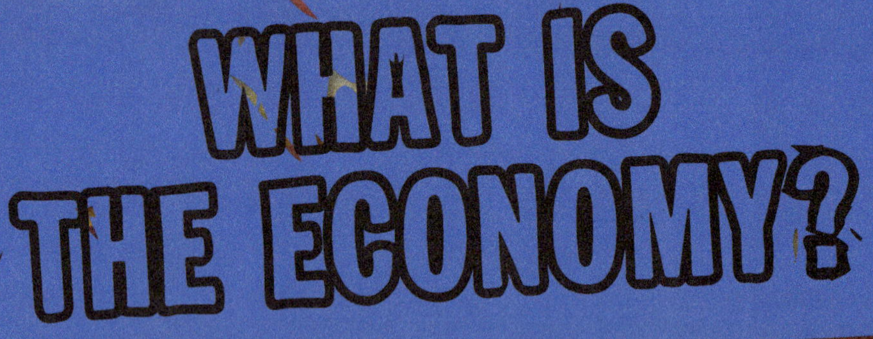

WHAT IS THE ECONOMY?

If you watch or read the news, you'll hear about the country's economy. An economy is all the ways money is made and used. It has to do with how people make, sell, and buy goods and services.

MAKE THE GRADE

Goods are objects that people buy, such as toys. Services are actions that people pay for, such as teaching.

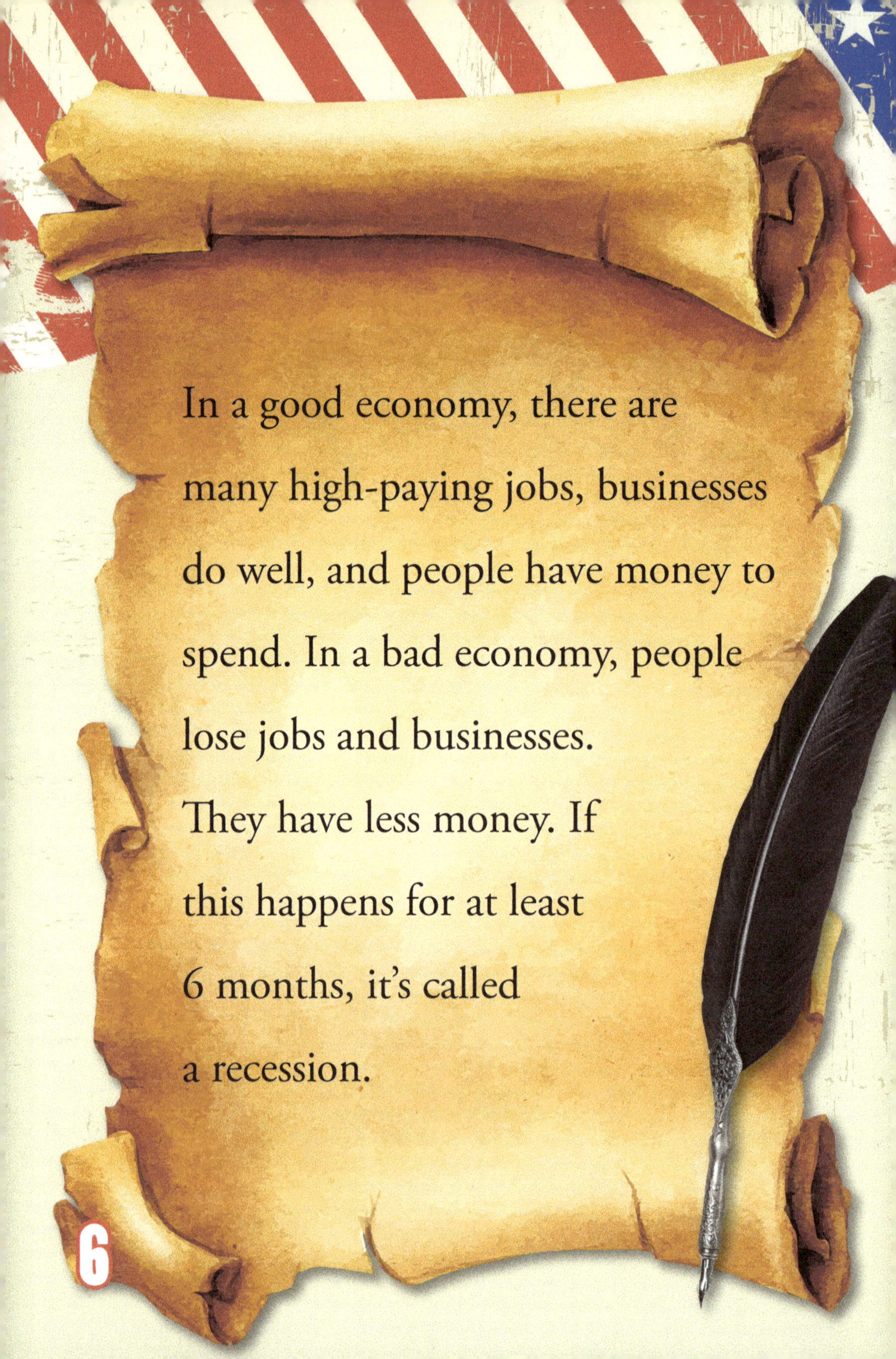

In a good economy, there are many high-paying jobs, businesses do well, and people have money to spend. In a bad economy, people lose jobs and businesses. They have less money. If this happens for at least 6 months, it's called a recession.

MAKE THE GRADE

It's normal for an economy to grow and contract, or become smaller, at different times.

FROM RECESSION TO DEPRESSION

Sometimes, a recession can become **severe**. The bad economy lasts a longer time, and people suffer in many ways. This is called a depression. The famous depression in US history began in 1929. It's called the Great Depression.

MAKE THE GRADE

A recession or depression can happen for many reasons. These include wars and too many or too few goods being produced.

THE ROARING TWENTIES

In the 1920s, many people grew richer by buying stocks, which are shares in a company's ownership. As a company's success grows, the price of its stock goes up. Some people even took out **loans** to buy stocks.

MAKE THE GRADE

The stock exchange, or stock market, is the buying and selling of stocks and **bonds**. It's also the place where this happens, like the New York Stock Exchange.

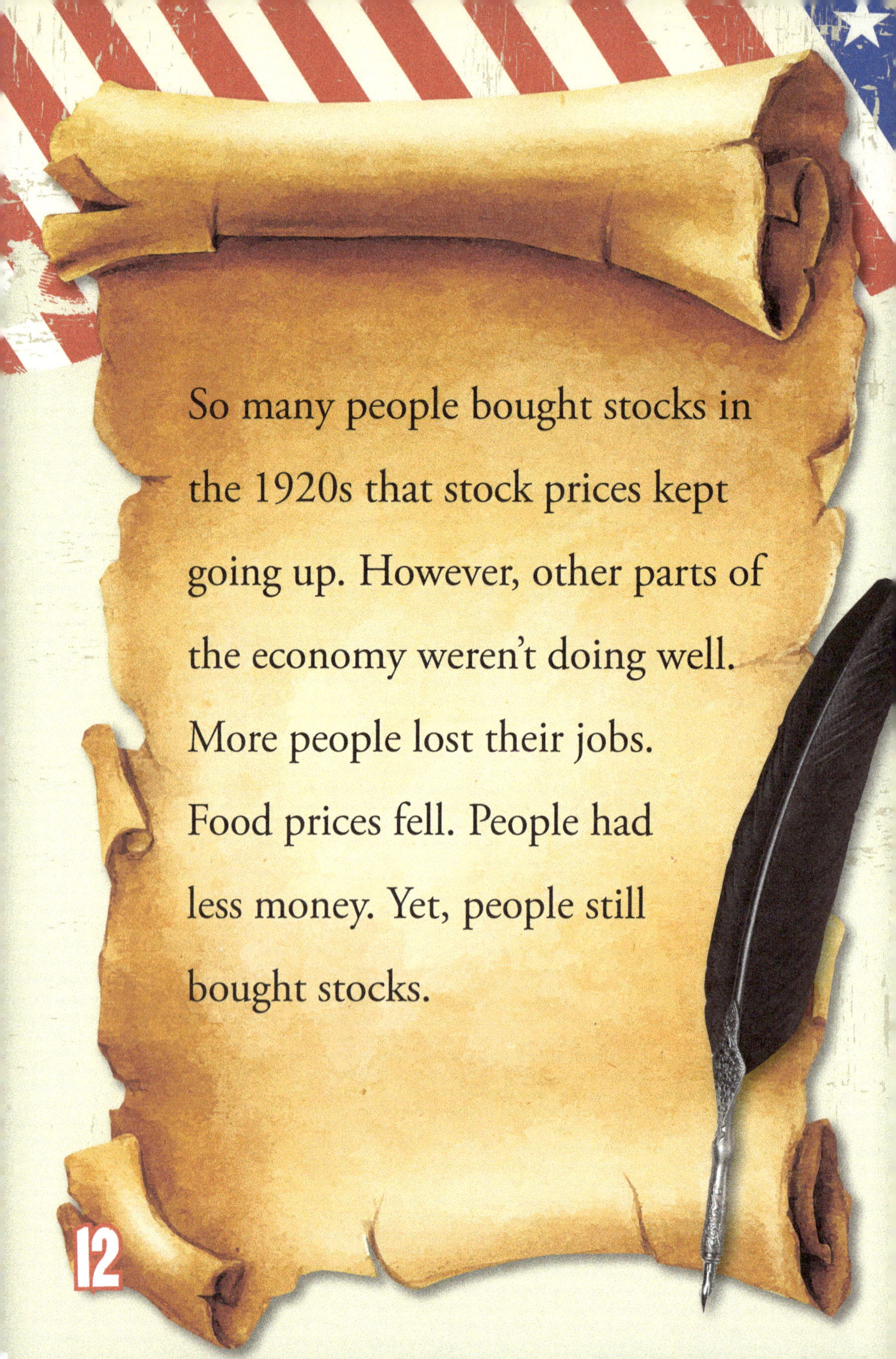

So many people bought stocks in the 1920s that stock prices kept going up. However, other parts of the economy weren't doing well. More people lost their jobs. Food prices fell. People had less money. Yet, people still bought stocks.

MAKE THE GRADE

People bought stocks because they hoped they could sell them for more money.

THE STOCK MARKET CRASH

Stock prices rose higher than they were worth. In September 1929, they began to fall. People rushed to sell stocks before they lost more value. On October 24, 1929, around 13 million shares of stock were sold. The stock market crash began.

TWO CENTS

STOCK VALUES CRASH IN RECORD STAMPEDE; BANKERS HALT ROUT

CURIOUS JAM WALL STREET TO SEE THE 'SHOW'

Huge Crowd Throngs "Money Lane" Seeking Thrill in Battle of Bulls and Bears

Butcher, Baker and Candlestick Maker Rush to View "World Series" of Finance

From The Inquirer Bureau.

NEW YORK, Oct. 24.—Huge crowds in a holiday mood resembling a confetti of faces from the upper stories of Wall Street skyscrapers surged up and down the narrow

...ers, housewives, truck drivers, teamsters, longshoremen from the nearby docks, bus conductors, collegians, as well as the butcher, baker and candlestick maker were in the mob hoping to see a world series of finance enacted before their eyes. Prosaic truth ... Wild rumors were

Stock Slump Fails to Dim Tax Cut Hope

WASHINGTON, Oct. 24 (A. P.).—The view that the recent slumps in the stock market will not affect the administration's tax-reduction programme is held by Treasury officials.

The officials regard the slumps as being more in paper profits than in actual values and believe the action was in the nature of a readjustment of the market and that stock prices generally still were above those paid by people who bought them at ordinary stages some time ago.

BUSINESS OF NATION UNSHAKEN, DECLARE TREASURY OFFICIALS

Probe Wall Street

Special to The Inquirer.

WASHINGTON, Oct. 24.—Amid renewed demand from Capitol Hill for an investigation of Wall Street, the Federal Reserve System and the causes of one of the worst stock market

UPSWING ENDS WILD SELLING IN 12,894,650 DAY

N. Y. Exchange Sees Most Violent Drop in Prices Since 1914; Ticker Hours Late

Market Rallies as Morgan and Other Financial Groups Meet and Issue Statement Declaring Trade Sound

From The Inquirer Bureau.

NEW YORK, Oct. 24.—Long withheld buying powers and the reassuring statements of America's most powerful banking interests came to the support ...ck market today and

never before equaled in volume, rapidity of fluctuations and ... reporting services.

When the final check-up ... completed late in the evening it ... found that 12,894,650 shares had been traded during the day's session.

Profits Disappear

MAKE THE GRADE

Days later, on October 29, 1929, over 16 million more shares of stock were sold. This was called Black Tuesday. Stock prices fell even more.

BANKS FAIL

During that time, people lost trust in banks. They tried to take out all their money. Many banks didn't have enough money on hand for everyone. They had used money for loans and **investments**. One-fifth of all US banks failed by 1933.

MAKE THE GRADE

Another reason banks failed is that people couldn't pay back loans they had taken out.

BUSINESSES FAIL

Because people had less money, they bought fewer goods. Businesses that made goods slowed **production** or shut down. More people lost their jobs. By 1933, 15 million Americans were out of work. Those who had jobs earned less money.

MAKE THE GRADE

During the Great Depression, **droughts** and dust storms hit the Great Plains. Farms couldn't grow crops. Millions moved, but couldn't find jobs.

LIFE DURING THE DEPRESSION

The Great Depression meant great **poverty** for millions of Americans. When people lost their jobs, whole families suffered and often went hungry. Those who had nothing to eat stood in long lines for free bread, soup, and other foods.

MAKE THE GRADE

During this time, the United States bought fewer goods from other nations and loaned them less money. The Great Depression spread to other countries.

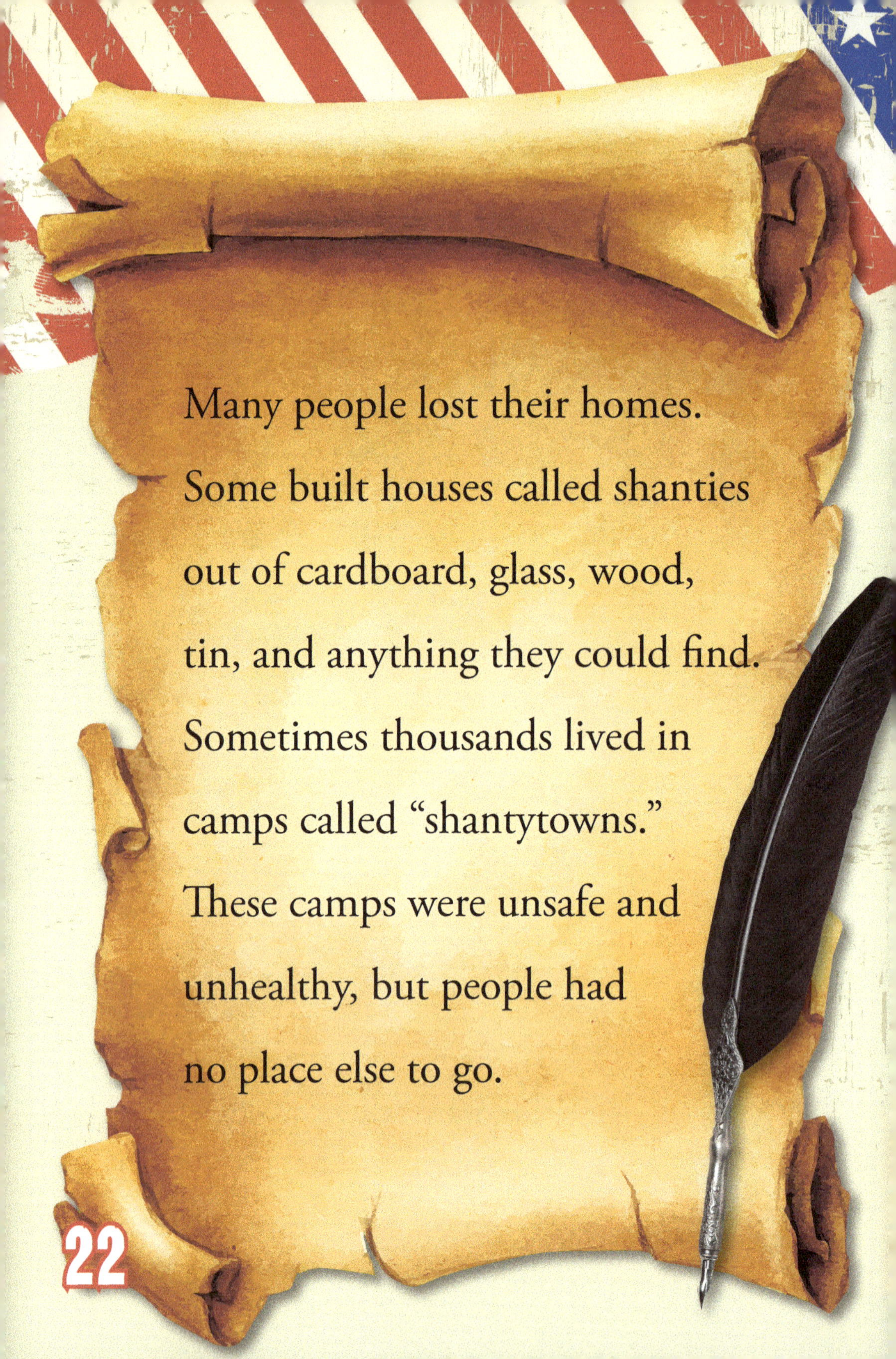

Many people lost their homes. Some built houses called shanties out of cardboard, glass, wood, tin, and anything they could find. Sometimes thousands lived in camps called "shantytowns." These camps were unsafe and unhealthy, but people had no place else to go.

MAKE THE GRADE

Many blamed US president Herbert Hoover for the depression or thought he didn't do enough to stop it. They called shantytowns Hoovervilles.

FROM HOOVER TO ROOSEVELT

The **federal** government under Herbert Hoover tried to help the economy. However, life didn't get better fast enough. In 1933, Franklin D. Roosevelt became US president. He began a **program** called the New Deal to fight the Great Depression.

MAKE THE GRADE

One of the first things Roosevelt did was close the banks until the government was sure they wouldn't fail.

THE NEW DEAL

The New Deal created millions of jobs. For example, the Civilian Conservation Corps and the Public Works Administration put people to work planting trees and building bridges. The Works Progress Administration's workers built roads, schools, and airports.

MAKE THE GRADE

Another part of the New Deal was the Social Security Act. It provided a **pension** for older people and those who were **disabled**.

SLOW RECOVERY

Slowly, the United States began to come out of the Great Depression. The country didn't **recover** completely until after it entered World War II in 1941. Americans joined the **military** or worked in factories making things needed for the war.

MAKE THE GRADE

The United States has never had another depression. The federal government acts when the economy falls into a recession to help prevent, or stop, a depression.

KEY DATES OF THE GREAT DEPRESSION

1929

The stock market begins to crash in October when millions of stocks are sold.

1930

People start taking large amounts of money out of banks until the banks begin to fail.

1932

Franklin D. Roosevelt is elected US president.

1933

Roosevelt closes banks until they're considered healthy enough to reopen.

1934

The Securities and Exchange Commission (SEC) is created to oversee stock market practices.

1935

The Social Security Act is passed. Other New Deal programs put people to work.

1936

Roosevelt is reelected president.

1939

World War II begins.

1941

The United States enters World War II and the economy improves.

GLOSSARY

bond: a paper that shows a government or company promises to pay back an amount of money that it has borrowed with interest, or more money

disabled: being unable to do some of the tasks of daily life

drought: a long period of very dry weather

federal: having to do with the national government

investment: something someone buys hoping it will increase in value

loan: money given to someone that must be paid back

military: the armed forces

pension: money paid by a company or government to someone old or sick who no longer works

poverty: the state of being poor

production: the action of making or growing something to sell it

program: a plan of things done in order to get a certain result

recover: to return to a normal state after a hard time

severe: very bad or serious

FOR MORE INFORMATION

Books

Lusted, Marcia Amidon. *The Great Depression: Experience the 1930s from the Dust Bowl to the New Deal.* White River Junction, VT: Nomad Press, 2016.

Pascal, Janet B. *What Was the Great Depression?* New York, NY: Grosset & Dunlap, 2015.

Websites

History Stories
www.history.com/news/life-for-the-average-family-during-the-great-depression
Find out more about life during the Great Depression.

US History: The Great Depression
www.ducksters.com/history/us_1900s/great_depression.php
Read more interesting facts about the Great Depression.

INDEX